Genre  Expository Text

MW00570374

**Essential Question**
What are the positive and negative effects
of new technology?

## What About

BY YVONNE MORRIN

We use technology every day in all aspects of our lives. Machines transport us, wash our clothes, keep our food fresh, help us communicate, and entertain us. Our lives would be very different if we didn't use technology!

Technology is advancing all the time. Although some people are excited about these changes, others are worried about them. What do you think could be some of the positive effects of new technology, and what might be some negative effects?

One area of technology that is advancing rapidly is **robotics**. There are millions of robots in the world doing jobs that are considered too dangerous or too boring for humans. The Mitsubishi Research Institute in Japan predicts that each household will own at least one robot by 2020. Many people think robots are useful to individuals and society. Others believe that people might become too dependent on robots or that robots might take over their jobs. Imagine being replaced by a robot!

Before forming an opinion about robotics, it is important to study the facts. Then you can weigh the advantages and the disadvantages. This helps you to make thoughtful and knowledgeable conclusions. It also allows you to cite evidence that backs up your reasoning and supports your opinion.

Technology affects many aspects of our lives.

# CHAPTER 1

# What Is a Robot?

The word *robot* comes from the Czech word *robota*, which means "forced labor." The word was first used in the 1920s in a play that featured mechanical workers who performed jobs in place of humans.

There are many definitions of what a robot is. One definition is that a robot is a machine that operates automatically in place of a human to complete a task. This definition would fit a washing machine. It carries out the task of washing clothes, taking the place of a human washing those clothes by hand. However, most people would not consider a washing machine to be a robot.

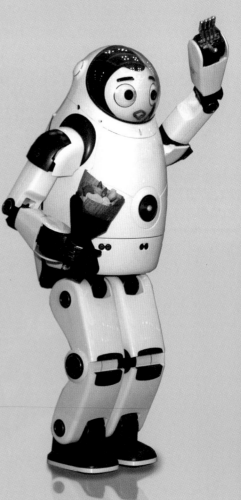

Robots come in many shapes and sizes.

A more accurate definition is that a robot is a machine that uses information from its surroundings to make decisions about what to do. The machine interacts with its environment to achieve a goal.

This kind of robot acts as if it has intelligence. It has equipment, such as cameras or microphones, to take in information. It also has a computer that responds to the information and makes decisions. Then the mechanical parts of the robot pick up and move objects.

**1495** Leonardo da Vinci designs an anthrobot, a mechanical man.

**1772** Swiss inventors Pierre and Henri Jacquet-Droz build an automated doll that can write messages with up to 40 characters.

**1898** Nikola Tesla demonstrates the first remote-controlled vehicles.

**1954** George Devol designs the first programmable robot.

**1966** Shakey, the first mobile robot controlled by artificial intelligence, is developed.

**1990** A walking robot called the Ambler is developed to operate in rugged terrain.

**2000** Humanoid robots and a robot dog are developed.

# Robots Through History

Between 1700 and 1900, a number of inventors created **automatons**, which looked like life-sized people or animals and had moving parts. Some automatons could play musical instruments and draw pictures. In 1739, Jacques Vaucanson built a Digesting Duck, an automaton that imitated the process of eating and digesting food. It could also imitate paddling. However, because automatons do not process any information about their environments, they are not considered true robots.

The first decision-making machine was built in 1911. It played chess against humans by using electrical **sensors** to figure out where the playing pieces were. Then it moved a mechanical arm to take its turn and move the chess pieces. Ten years later, another version used magnets underneath the board to move the pieces.

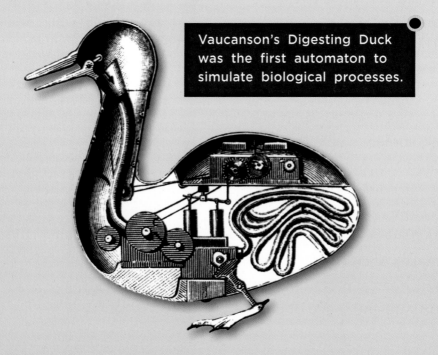

Vaucanson's Digesting Duck was the first automaton to simulate biological processes.

Photos 12/Alamy

# FICTIONAL ROBOTS

Long before real robots were invented, science fiction stories included robots. Some of the movies of the 1920s and 1930s showed robots plotting to take over Earth! Later, when robots came to television in the 1950s and 1960s, they were often shown as helpful companions.

A 1926 film, *Metropolis*, featured a robot called Maria. She is thought to have been the precursor to the robot C-3PO in the *Star Wars* movies.

Then, in the mid-twentieth century, computer technology developed to the point where machines could be controlled by **artificial** brains. These machines are considered to be the first true robots.

In the 1940s, William Grey Walter developed the first machines that were able to move freely and interact with their environments. They rolled around on three wheels and could make decisions about how to avoid objects. Because of their shape and slow movements, the machines were called Elsie the Tortoise and Elmer the Tortoise.

# CHAPTER 2

# Robots at Work

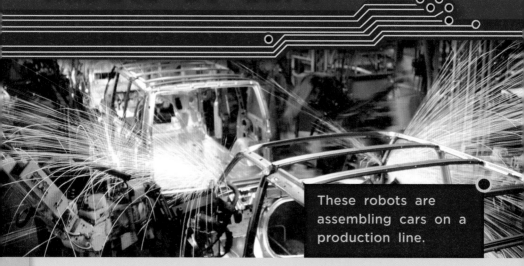

These robots are assembling cars on a production line.

The first robot designed to work in a factory had a heavy lifting arm. Its movements were controlled by **electronics**. The robot could be programmed to perform different actions. In 1961, the robot was used in a factory that built cars, lifting metal parts that were too hot for humans to handle. Robots began to be used more widely in American factories in the 1960s and 1970s. In the 1970s, more advanced, computer-controlled electric arms guided by sensors were developed. Since the 1990s, small electric arms have been used in laboratories, where they perform intricate tasks.

Although robots are expensive, they can save a company a lot of money over time. That's because they:

- can often do jobs faster and more accurately than a human can;
- don't get tired and make mistakes;
- don't need breaks to eat, drink, or sleep;
- don't get bored by repeating the same task many times.

Because these robots changed the way things were being done in factories, some people worried that robots would replace people and take their jobs. They also worried about safety. In 1988, some incorrectly programmed robots at a factory began smashing car windshields and painting each other!

Although industrial robots first appeared in the United States, the **manufacture** of most robots moved to Japan and Europe in the 1980s. Japan has an aging population, and people were concerned that there would not be enough young workers in the future. They thought robots would be needed to do many jobs. Japan now has a higher ratio of robots to workers than any other country.

## INDUSTRIAL ROBOT LOCATIONS

Asia leads the world in robot use.

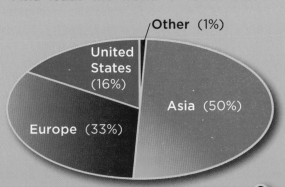

Other (1%)

United States (16%)

Asia (50%)

Europe (33%)

VIEWPOINTS
**ROBOTS IN THE WORKPLACE**

"I think having robots at work is a good idea. They can do all the dangerous jobs."

"If we start using robots instead of humans at work, will I lose my job and be replaced by a machine?"

What do you think? Is it a good idea to have robots in the workplace?

# Too Dangerous for Humans!

Robots can be used for many jobs that are dangerous for humans. They can clean up chemical spills and toxic waste in nuclear plants, monitor the amount of oil in an environment after an oil spill, and even **defuse** bombs.

Robots can also be used following natural disasters, such as earthquakes or floods. There are many dangers after such events. There may be fires or gas leaks, or damaged walls could collapse and people could be trapped. In these situations, the rescuers who search for survivors put their own lives at risk. Robotic scouts were developed to perform searches and make rescuing survivors safer.

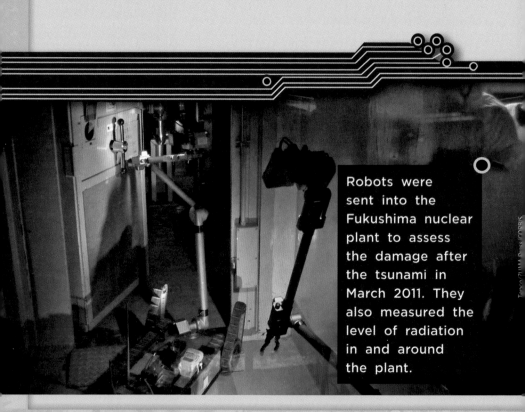

Robots were sent into the Fukushima nuclear plant to assess the damage after the tsunami in March 2011. They also measured the level of radiation in and around the plant.

Robotic scouts can access dangerous areas or areas that are difficult to get to. They can carry equipment such as cameras and gas detectors that can send important information back to the rescuers. These data help rescuers as they do an analysis of the situation and make plans for a recovery mission. Robots can carry food, medicine, air tanks, and two-way radios to survivors who are unable to move. Some robots are even designed to drag survivors out of wreckage.

Space is another risky environment for humans. Engineers have developed a robotic astronaut, called a robonaut. This robot can roll over the surface of planets exploring the **terrain** and pick up samples with its mechanical hands. A robonaut can use the same workspace and tools as a human. However, unlike a human, this robot doesn't need to breathe, eat, or keep warm.

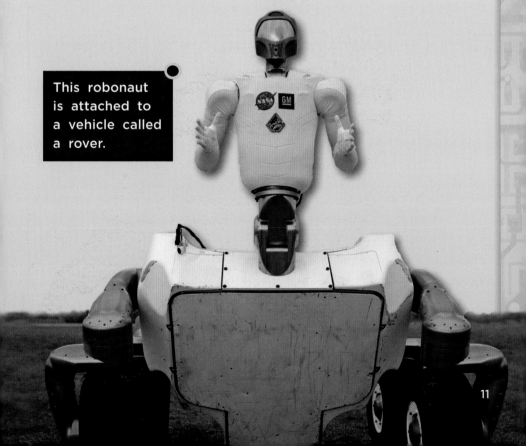

This robonaut is attached to a vehicle called a rover.

# CHAPTER 3

# New Uses for Robots

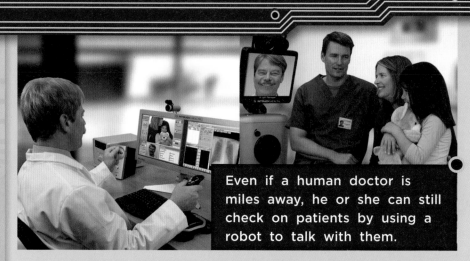

Even if a human doctor is miles away, he or she can still check on patients by using a robot to talk with them.

As scientists develop more advanced technology, new uses are being found for robots.

## Robots in Hospitals

Many hospitals now use robots to help care for patients and perform basic tasks. Robots can do a variety of jobs, such as delivering food and equipment or dispensing medicine. Using robots reduces the risk of disease and infection spreading. Robots also free up nurses and other staff to perform other jobs.

However, there are drawbacks to using robots for patient care. Some people are frightened by robots, and others don't trust them to get things right. Many patients feel more comfortable interacting with another human rather than with a machine. To make them more appealing to children, some robots used in children's wards have been covered in fur or built to look like toys.

InTouch Health

## SURGICAL ROBOT OPERATIONS

This graph shows that the number of operations performed by one brand of surgical robot increased every year between 2005 and 2010. More growth is predicted.

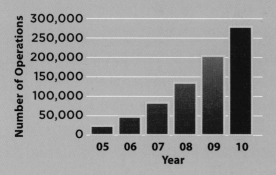

Surgical robots are becoming increasingly popular, too. Human surgeons control the surgical robots. Humans use these robots to perform complex operations such as heart operations, brain surgery, and kidney transplants.

A surgical robot can be more precise than a human surgeon. A robot doesn't have big hands and fingers, and it needs less room to manipulate surgical instruments. Consequently, it can make a smaller cut in a patient. This means patients have less pain, a smaller scar, and fewer infections. As a result, patients heal faster.

## VIEWPOINTS
## ROBOTIC NURSING ASSISTANTS

Japan has a large elderly population living in nursing homes. Some elderly people like the idea of robotic nursing assistants, but others don't.

"I don't like having a robot deliver my pills. I don't trust the robot to get it right. I'm lonely and I would prefer to talk to a real person."

"It's good that the robots deliver my meals. It means nurses have more time to look after the people who need attention."

What do you think? Would you be comfortable with a robot nurse?

"Robots might be able to solve almost all of our environmental problems. We should spend more money on developing new robots to clean up the environment."

"Until we can produce robots in a more environmentally friendly way, we shouldn't make more. Spend money on preventing environmental problems first."

What do you think? Are robots good or bad for the environment?

## Friend of the Environment?

Many people are wary of society's increasing use of robots. They also feel that robots are environmentally unfriendly. They say that robots are made out of **minerals** that need to be mined, and that mining can damage the environment. They argue that the factories that make robots use natural **resources**, such as fuel and water, and that this adds to a drain on the environment. In addition, opponents of robots say that throwing away outdated technology from robots, such as old computers, can harm the environment and contribute to the increasing amount of waste.

Computers contain poisonous chemicals that must be disposed of carefully because they can harm the environment.

This type of robot floats on the surface of the ocean and cleans up oil that is harmful to marine life.

However, the counterpoint is that robots can be very helpful to the environment. Engineers are inventing robots that can be used to check the health of the environment by measuring toxins and cleaning up **pollutants**. Some robots use an eco-friendly power source, such as solar panels, which collect energy from the sun. One robot can even detect and capture slugs and then turn them into fuel!

The future might be full of robots helping to return the environment to a natural state. Already people have designed robots that can sort different types of plastic for recycling. Other robots can plant trees, using steam to power the robot and to kill weeds. Another type of robot can move around and filter pollution out of the air.

# Learning from Animals

What is intelligence? Some people think intelligence means being **logical** and good at analyzing data or solving math puzzles. Now many believe intelligence means being able to cope and make decisions in response to any change in the environment.

Animals are very good at adapting to their environments and surviving in them. Instead of trying to develop artificial intelligence and make robots more human-like, many engineers are now turning to animals for ideas.

One example is a rat-robot that can operate in the dark or in very dusty conditions. The rat-robot has touch sensors in its whiskers, cameras in its eye sockets, and tiny microphones in its ears. Its inventor says, "We want to make robots that are able to look after themselves." The rat-robot can be used in smoke-filled rooms or even underground to help find and rescue people.

There are also robots that have many legs so that they can walk easily and quickly over rough ground like a spider does. Others can hover like a hummingbird.

The rat-robot is small enough to fit into places humans can't easily go. In poor light, it can use its whiskers to sense where to go.

Some people feel uncomfortable around robots that look too human, so companies make different styles of robots, including some that look like animals.

In the future, inventors are likely to improve robots and come up with many new uses for them. More robots will care for the sick and provide companionship to lonely people. They will solve environmental problems, help in disasters, and make workplaces safer. For all these reasons, many people will develop positive opinions about the work robots do.

However, there will still be people who don't approve of robots. These people might fear that we will start to rely on robots too much and that humans will lose important skills, such as how to relate to other humans. Other people might feel uncomfortable around robots. They might prefer to interact with another person rather than with a machine.

When companies design new robots, they will have to consider all of these opinions in order to make robots that people will be willing to use.

# Respond to Reading

## Summarize

Use details from the text to summarize the positive and negative effects of robots. Your graphic organizer may help you.

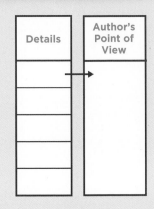

| Details | Author's Point of View |
|---------|------------------------|
|         |                        |
|         |                        |
|         |                        |
|         |                        |

## Text Evidence

**1.** What features of *What About Robots?* tell you it is an expository text? **GENRE**

**2.** What point of view does the author reveal in Chapter 3 of *What About Robots?* What details from the text support this? **AUTHOR'S POINT OF VIEW**

**3.** The Greek prefix *auto-* means "self" or "same." Using this and context clues, figure out the meaning of *automatically* on page 4. Then find another word in the text that has this prefix and explain its meaning. **GREEK AND LATIN PREFIXES**

**4.** Write about the author's position on robots. Do you think the author is pro-robot or anti-robot? Use evidence from the text to support your answer. **WRITE ABOUT READING**

## Compare Texts
Read an argument against using robots.

# No Substitute

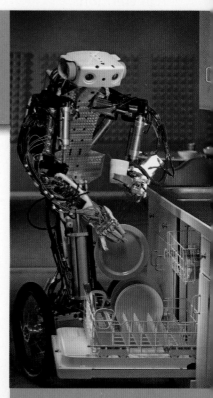

This robot was designed to help around the house.

Some people say that in the future, every home will have a robot. The robot could be a companion for someone who is lonely, or it could be a servant to do the housework. Many people think this will be a wonderful use of technology. They say it will free up time for busy people and make their lives better. In this essay, I hope to persuade you that a robot in every home would actually be a terrible thing.

People who rely on a machine to do household chores will soon become lazy and lose many skills. Children who don't have to do chores while growing up might never learn the value or satisfaction of hard work. By not taking responsibility for messes that they have created, humans might stop taking responsibility for their actions.

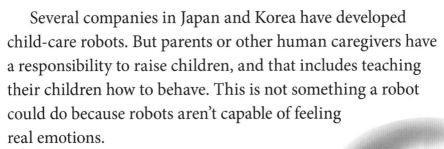

Several companies in Japan and Korea have developed child-care robots. But parents or other human caregivers have a responsibility to raise children, and that includes teaching their children how to behave. This is not something a robot could do because robots aren't capable of feeling real emotions.

A robot can't interact with children the same way a human does. It can't show **compassion**, sympathy, or love. Children raised by a robot might not fully develop their emotions and could find it difficult to respond to other humans.

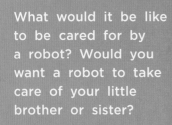

What would it be like to be cared for by a robot? Would you want a robot to take care of your little brother or sister?

There are safety issues to consider too. A robot could cause damage in the home or serious injury to people. Robots are only able to do what they are programmed to do. This means that a robot could do something dangerous if something unexpected happened. In an emergency, the robot might not respond at all, or it could respond inappropriately if it were not programmed to deal with the problem.

If something went wrong while a robot was in charge, whose fault would it be? Would it be the fault of the robot, the robot's programmer, the robot's user, or the robot's owner?

Finally, what would happen to all the human workers the robots would replace? Many people work as house cleaners, babysitters, or nurse companions. If robots took over this work, many people would lose their jobs.

For all of these reasons, it is clear that a robot in every home is not a good idea.

## Make Connections

What does *No Substitute* identify as the negative effects of using robots? ESSENTIAL QUESTION

After reading both texts, what is your point of view about robots? TEXT TO TEXT

# Glossary

**artificial** *(ahr-tuh-FISH-uhl)* not natural; made by humans *(page 7)*

**automatons** *(aw-TOM-uh-tonz)* machines that follow a specific set of instructions; some look like humans or animals *(page 6)*

**compassion** *(kuhm-PASH-uhn)* a deep feeling of sympathy for someone else and a strong desire to help *(page 20)*

**defuse** *(dee-FYEWZ)* remove the fuse from a bomb so that it can't explode *(page 10)*

**electronics** *(i-lek-TRON-iks)* electrical circuits, devices, and equipment *(page 8)*

**logical** *(LOJ-i-kuhl)* connecting facts or events in a reasonable way *(page 16)*

**manufacture** *(man-yuh-FAK-chuhr)* the making or producing of something *(page 9)*

**minerals** *(MIN-uhr-uhlz)* naturally occurring substances, usually obtained from soil or rock *(page 14)*

**pollutants** *(puh-LEW-tuhnts)* things that are harmful to the environment *(page 15)*

**resources** *(REE-sawrs-iz)* things that are useful to humans, such as water, fuel, and food *(page 14)*

**robotics** *(roh-BOT-iks)* the branch of technology that deals with how robots are built and used *(page 3)*

**sensors** *(SEN-suhrz)* devices that can detect things, such as movement or light *(page 6)*

**terrain** *(tuh-RAYN)* the surface of the land *(page 11)*

# Index

# Focus on Science

**Purpose** To explore what robots can and cannot do

## Procedure

**Step 1** Use the Internet to research current developments in robotics and learn more about what robots can and cannot do.

**Step 2** Make a two-column chart labeled "Can" and "Cannot." As you learn more about robots, record what they can and cannot do on your chart.

**Step 3** Now make a chart for humans and record what humans can and cannot do.

**Step 4** After conducting your research, how do you feel about robots versus humans? Use information from your charts to create a poster, a slide presentation, or a skit that compares robots with humans. Make sure you clearly show your point of view.

**Conclusion** Do you think the use of robots will become more common, less common, or stay about the same as it is now? Why?